Schizophrenia

Schizophrenia

The Voices, they won't let me go . . .

or will they?

By: Katie Hartwig

authorHOUSE®

AuthorHouse™
1663 Liberty Drive
Bloomington, IN 47403
www.authorhouse.com
Phone: 1-800-839-8640

Published by AuthorHouse   03/12/2013

ISBN: 978-1-4817-2620-7 (sc)
ISBN: 978-1-4817-2619-1 (e)

Library of Congress Control Number: 2013904430

Contents

Dedication vii

Introduction ix

Prayer 1

"My Job" 2

"Taunting Chatter" 4

"Faces" 6

"Normal Visions" 8

"To The Doctor" 9

"Distraught" 11

"A Friend" 13

"Thoughts" 15

"Spiritual Visits" 18

"Angry Outbursts" 20

"Idol Hands" 22

"I cry" 23

"My Stories" 25

My Story 26

My Story Two 27

My Story Three 28

My Story Four 29

My Story Five 30

My Story Six 31

My Story Seven 33

"Beautiful Smile" 34

"Suicide" 37

"Pep Talk" 40

"Pep Talk Two" 42

"Pep Talk Three" 43

"Pep Talk for smokers" 44

"Pep talk for those who are suicidal" 45

"Critical" 47

"Another Kind of Serenity Prayer"—"The Courage Prayer" 49

"Schizophrenia The Other Side" 51

"Encouragement" 52

"My Voices" 53

"KEEP SEEKING A DOCTOR" 54

"Instruction" 56

"Dear Friend why suicide" 57

"Buck naked" 58

"Yeah I sinned" 60

"Accuser of the brethren" 61

"Let Me Be" 63

"Making my delusions work for me at my job" 65

"Working with My Dad" 67

Letter to a friend or relative 68

A Song 69

"A Prayer" 70

Dedication

This book is dedicated to my family and friends. A special thank you to my Mom and my sister who have been my support system outside of Community Mental Health (CMH). And special memorial to my Dad for his insight and love, even while he was so sick. Thank you to CMH, to hospitals and group homes as well.

I love you all,

Katie

Introduction

This book is about schizophrenia. It has been written by a person who has paranoid schizophrenia. Life has been hard for me, though, I am now living with managed schizophrenia. And I have been successfully working now for six years and fourteen days and counting.

I wanted to write a book to share with my friends and those who may not yet be my friends. Those who know a person with schizophrenia may like to read to see what helped me or what didn't help me so they may help their loved one. Those with schizophrenia may feel comforted that they are not alone, that someone cares and has been there. Maybe you too will find guidance for your life—A little help to bring you along to where you one day will be able to manage your schizophrenia as well.

You will find that it is repetitious at points but I wanted to stress those things that did help in my healing. Things that brought me from unmanaged schizophrenia to managed.
God bless you one and all. As only through Him will we all be totally freed!

Katie

Prayer

Our Father, who art in Heaven
Hallowed be thy name . . .

Father, be with us all, everyone in the great world, of Yours. Lead each and every one of us, so we may all be the people that You desire us to be.

Be with our rulers LORD, where ever they may be; At home, school, business, those holding an office, managers in factories, fast food restaurants, those in the military, those in sports; all leaders Everywhere. LORD, Let them rule with love and with peace.

Be with each person that is reading this book
That they would glean from it what they need
That they will find comfort and healing
And let your mighty hand continue to uphold them
As only You can do.

We thank you LORD for Your love.

We pray all this in the mighty name of Jesus.

Amen and amen!

"My Job"

Well I work. Isn't that amazing! I have paranoid schizophrenia and I am working. Oh, there was a time I couldn't work. I'd run from place to place, fearful of every living human I ran into and I'd run some more.

But now, I Work! It isn't a glamorous job or a sophisticated job, but a job just the same. I am a machine operator. I make air bag cannons. I am pretty proud of what I do. Eight and a half years ago I couldn't thin long enough to function in any kind of job.

I make small tubing parts in a small town about 40 minutes from my home. That in itself is pretty amazing too. I drive 40 minutes there, and 40 minutes home. Actually right now I am brazing too. I work with fire! Wow! If you know someone with schizophrenia you know what a feat this really and truly is.

I clock in on a time clock that reads my hand. Technology is just wonderful. Yet again, eight and a half years ago I would have thought that machine was the work of the devil and I would have run from it for sure. I would have been terrified I was taking "the number" and ran 90 miles an hour away from that puppy. Now it is just a machine that keeps track of my hours and I get a pay check through it. Happy me! I no longer have to depend totally on others to take care of me.

I have been teaching others how to braze too. I had someone teach me at work. Boy it was scary, a torch! But I wanted to have a job that would be more secure so I didn't say anything, I just let him teach me and kept smiling. And it worked. I know how to adjust a torch to make the heat at a level that is right for me. And I am teaching others!

Schizophrenic people can do things. It takes us longer to learn. But it is possible to learn. I know most people say schizophrenic people never get better and they only get worse. I do not believe that. I believe they need more support, someone to walk beside them. At times a group of people to watch over them. And that is not bad. Some people are just not meant to take care of themselves. But with the right support, a person with schizophrenia will be able to work in time. Really, they will. But they definitely need time before they can do most things on their own.

Just recently I was promoted too. I work in the tool crib doing inventory. I input information into the computer and keep track of the supplies. In time I will be back to machine operator part time and crib attendant the other half. I am so grateful to God and all those who stood by me to get me this far in life.

"Taunting Chatter"

Word for word
Condemnation.

Exile.
Loneliness.
Fear.

Over and over
Day for day

Nothing I say
No where to go

I've tried
I've cried
I'm still here

Taunting voices
Go Away
I do not want to hear
Leave me alone
Go Away
It is none of my business
Leave me alone.
I don't care, it is none of my business
Leave me alone.

"Taunting Chatter" was written to explain how I talked to the voices I use to hear and, at stressful times, may still hear. To confront the voices and tell them to go away helped me to get control over those voices. Jesus said to reverse curses. I thought about that for a time and I decided saying "not so, God bless you" was a very good way to reverse them.

At first I was reversing curses every 30 seconds, over and over all day long. I got bolder and started saying "Not so leave me alone, I don't care to hear that, leave me alone in Jesus name." Now I did not say these things out loud, I had my share of lock ups; and knew that would just put me back in. My visits to the psychiatric ward were plenty before I was able to uncover these truths in the bible and to speak them inside myself. Being direct to the voices and adamant that I did not care to hear, brought me peace from these voices.

Sometimes now when things are scary for me I might have to fall back and use this type of confrontation to get away from these voices or fears that they may be.

As time goes by, these voices are less and less and it becomes second hand and I do it without even knowing I am.

Don't lose heart, God loves you my dear friend, and you too can get past your voices and live a more fuller life.

"Faces"

Faces found in a rug?
Animated, some scary, some not
Some become my friends
Most my enemy
Coming out of carpet,
Of designs, curtains
Coming out floating in mid air
Just as I lye there
When I am awake or awakened
When I'm asleep
Every where.
To what seems to me life.
Why are they here?

Real faces speak to me,
To you.
But can you find them
Can you hear them
Do they speak
What will comfort
In the midst
Of all your strife.

For, that is what we need, comfort.
Comfort in the midst of our despair.
Someone to sit by us to just be there.

"Faces", was a reflection of where I had been. Of feeling no one understood me, turned into no one cares for me. Alone in the world fearful of everyone I met. I was drawn into a fantasy world. Listening to voices some that were planning to hurt me, to hurt my family. So much strife or despair turned me inward and a fantasy world of floating forms and people kept me trapped in a world that was not only devastating to me but to my family and close friends. People with schizophrenia care too much about others and themselves. Until they can see that, they are locked in this fearful world. That is where I was locked, until I felt cared about and could face the world again and not try to fix everyone around me.

Society thinks it is wrong to take care of people. That people ought to be able to stand by themselves. And people with schizophrenia are at the top of the list to be pushed to do for themselves.

In their defense, they need someone to walk along side of them and hold them up for as many years as possible to get them to a safe place where they can and will take care of themselves. Not saying they are not in a safe place but in their mind, as it was in my mind, they do not feel safe. So they are not, not until they can feel it.

Trying to focus on what is real a table, a chair, a person is so important to get past these visions as well.

"Normal Visions"

Now you wouldn't think
There is such a thing
But, yes there really is

Still visions?
Some when I awake
Floating forms along with
Racing heart beat
This is normal if
Your blood pressure
Is off, too high or low
And once you get your groundings
They are gone and your good to go

Still visions?
Anesthesia and some meds
Cause floating images
And yep that is normal
And they will go away too.

"Normal Visions" is a tribute to my Dad. He was very
sick and dying and I went in to see him and he talked
to me about anesthesia and how it causes people
to see floating images. He told me that it is ok, it is
normal. I learned by an article about blood pressure
causing visions too.

"To The Doctor"

Words ring out:
Take your meds.
Easy to say, not so easy to do.
Side affects: just terrible;
Causing pain unbelievable,
Highs "the world" envy's.
No way to live life.

The pill it did not work,
It caused so much pain
Non-belief from those in attendance:
Belittling remarks cutting deep:
You just don't want to take your meds.

Spinning in a world, so distraught
No one understands.
More confusion
More voices
More faces no one can see but me.

Can you help me:
Find the right med for me.
I really do want to be better.
Nothing I've tried has helped
Is there a right med for me?
Doctor?

"To the doctor" is a poem crying out for understanding. So many in the field of psychiatry believe that schizophrenic people just don't want to take their meds.

I suppose in a way that is true. Why would one want to take their meds if they caused them pain in their head and their butt cheeks, the size of a Charlie horse! Or one that has them hanging out the window of a fast food restaurant long after their customer has left. Seeing things and hearing voices is less fearful than all of that.

That is what happened to me on a couple of meds. Those were the worst so I remember them vividly. I took them and I wanted them to work and they didn't. I wrote this poem to "The Doctor", whoever they may be who is belittling their patient because they won't take their meds. I saw a lot when I was in hospitals and a group home. People look down on people with schizophrenia. When actually " the weak" ought to be taken care of.

I wanted in this poem for people to see that. To understand I and many other people with this disease do want to follow orders. Really!

And for the patient. Just because someone says something about you it doesn't mean it is true and it is ok for people to have their own opinion. It happens to everyone in life.

"Distraught"

Tears filled her eyes
The words within capture her mind;
Overflowing with grief.

No one sees:
She wants to take advantage of you.
Words cutting tears,
Cutting arms, taking some people lives.

She is a person who needs.
Needs more that most to stay alive.
(If you can work and don't work you should not eat":
That means some people are unable to work.
Don't judge her or him harshly or push them more.
Bringing:
Distraught
Fills her eyes,
    Her mind,
    Her life,
Till she is paralyzed
From simple life.

When, no one sees the need
They hear words of confusion.
Distraught over life.
And the cycle begins again
Locked up, unheard the cycle will go on and on.

Katie Hartwig

"Distraught" has a lot of meaning to it. So many people with schizophrenia are just that distraught. Many try to commit suicide and thankfully many survive. I think people with schizophrenia are people who need others to hold them up, to walk with them when they are down, to just listen to them. This poem was written to show how desperately we need someone to just be there for us and how alone we do feel.

It speaks to the height of fear that really does dwell within us. Fear of being alone. Fear of losing family. Fear of losing friends. All this fear leads schizophrenic people into despair.

For me I learned the most when I shared my thoughts and no one listened but they looked like they were. Oh my I told my whole family I must be Jesus reincarnated. Not a one said otherwise or chastened me. I just needed to say it I guess. Because now I know how silly that sounds and is.

I did a lot of crazy things and told my husband about them and he didn't say a word. I felt accepted. Later I found out when I was served with divorce papers, it was just because he didn't care. Funny I think that indifference was exactly what I needed so God blessed me with a 5 ½ year marriage with a man who did not care for me, so HE could heal me.

"A Friend"

I need you to just be my friend:
Listen.
Don't tell me what to do.

My words might be confused, disjointed, angry:
Just accept them as they are, listen.
Don't be concerned!:
That is a big one, but oh how I need it!

I need to say what is inside of me,
Let it out without judgment or fear from you:
You thinking "Oh my she thinks off the wall":
She needs an institution only takes away from me
(my existence).

Your silence will bring my peace.
I will not know it without.
I may not be right, but I will feel accepted.

Confined I will lose more:
I will continue to say, do and be confused more.
That is just how it is.

I know because that is what my husband gave to me
A listening ear, unconcerned! And that set me free.

Well "A friend" tells it all. How I needed to just be listened to. Like a young child babbles and their parents listen to them and accept them.

Somehow I got in this place where I can't control myself, my thoughts, my life. And I just need a friend to be there for me.

Sometimes I need more than one friend, I had Community Mental Health (CMH) and at times a group of professionals working with me. Most times one good friend helped me to learn to grow. Especially in their own silence and letting go of the fear they had for me and of me and my thoughts.

Sure if I am suicidal I need a hospital. If I'm reckless I need one too. But when I am just babbling about silly things. I really just need that unconcerned ear. That hand in mine to see me through all those crazy thoughts.

I went through that and after time went by, I realized, well that was really crazy. At the time though I felt confirmed. I felt accepted as a person. And that is what all of us need in this life isn't it. An open mind and a caring hand. A friend.

I saw so many people in CMH disciplined over and over and they only got worse, babbled more, got more confused. And they ended up staying in that confusion more. The weak need to be taken care of. Not disciplined.

"Thoughts"

Your going to fall down the stairs~~~
Your granddad did, it was your fault
Not so he had a heart attack.
Your going to fall down the stairs~~~
You caused your granddad to fall
It was all your fault you yelled at him
Years before he didn't understand
And it caused his death . . .
Not so he had a heart attack.
Your going to fall down the stairs~~~

1, 2, 3, 4, 5, 6, 7, 8, 9, 10, 11, 12, 13 . . .

Thoughts no more!

I can count you away!
It is a better day.
Besides, Jesus forgives us our sins . . .

John 3:17-18
For God sent the Son into the world, not to
condemn the world, but that the world might be
saved through Him. He who believes in Him is not
condemned . . .

So deceiver, BACK OFF! My past is my past, I
repented and it is covered under the blood of Jesus.

"Thoughts" is a poem about another way I have gotten past bad thoughts. I live in a house with my Mom, I pay rent! Too funny, I just wanted you to know that. Although she does cook and clean as working and doing both is hard for me still. Well I live up the stairs and most of my life I've been afraid of falling down those stairs.

One day as I was going up them I remembered what I did to help my fears of stairs as I grew up. I started counting the stairs as I went up. It was best to know exactly how many stairs. That way I knew when I had made it safely to the top. I count going down as well. I don't count out loud, just in my head and it works every time. If your putting something in your head, it pushes everything else out. :O)

I haven't really thought about reversing the curse in this area I suppose because it is a safety issue that is real. Counting really does help me. I sometimes get winded going up stairs and just that little extra push helps me to stay calm.

I think another good way to calming voices heard by schizophrenics is to say the alphabet in your head, maybe at first some people would need to say them out loud until they have the voices under control then they can do that in their head.

I'm a Christian with schizophrenia and reciting verses is an awesome way to getting rid of the ugly old voices. Some of those verses you will find within this book. An easy one is The 23rd Psalm.

"Spiritual Visits"

Spiritual visits are not unusual
A person may visit you spiritually
I read that in the bible
So I know it is true.

What to do?

Easy,
Tell the person
To go back to their body in the name of Jesus Christ.

They will go—Don't be scared
It is not unusual
It is just a fact of life we as schizophrenics
Know more then most

But after a time
You might not know it as well as it becomes second
hand
In your fight to stand up for what is right!

So say it with me now, go back to your body in the
name of Jesus Christ.

"Spiritual Visits" is a really good poem for healing. I read the bible a lot as most schizophrenic people do. I ran across some verses somewhere in there about spiritual visits. They really are real. And something that we need to attend to, just as the poem says. Tell the person to go back to their body in the name of Jesus Christ. There is no other name among men that we can be saved and there is no other name among men that can ship a nosey spirit back home!

At first, just like with the voices, I had to repeat this over and over. Not out loud but silently tell the person by name to go back to their body in the name of Jesus Christ.

I know this may sound crazy to the average person. But if you are a friend of a person with schizophrenia, you know they have probably spoken about it as well.

God is a good God and he put that in the bible for us to hear.
We can be saved in the name of Jesus and be delivered in that precious name as well.

"Angry Outbursts"

Don't leave me or abandon me
I am scared and alone
Afraid no one will take care of me
I scream
At the top of my lungs
I plead
I run down the hall
Banging the walls side to side
I scream
Fear holding me in terror
No one wants to take care of me
I would if I could
Fear takes hold of me
I scream
Angry words flying every where
Where will I go
Who will take care of me
Anger wells up
I scream
I scream
I scream
Can't you see
I need to be taken care of
I scream until I'm worn out
I scream

"Angry Outburst" we as schizophrenic people tend to have them. We are afraid. My husband wanted a divorce the first two years of marriage and I was petrified. I had given him all my furniture and sold my car for him and now he wanted to leave me. I was terrified. I screamed and screamed and screamed, until my voice was shot. He would just look at me. I did not know where I would go. How I would survive and I had them, those "angry outbursts". My husband just looked at me listened and let me run them out. After a time I got less fearful. And even in time I was able to handle the big "d" word, divorce, without screaming. But not without a lot of tears.

I believe from my own experience that most of the "angry outbursts" are from fear. Fear of being left alone and not knowing how to take care of myself. Schizophrenic people need someone who can care for their every need at times. And as I said that is not wrong. We are told to take care of the weak.

If it becomes to overwhelming for the caregiver they need to get help from hospitals and Community Mental Health and possibly group homes as well.

"Idol Hands"

Have you ever heard that "idol hands" are the "devils workshop". Confusion is of the devil not of Christ. I knew that from being a Christian.
Don't flip out here!

God is greater than anything the devil can do and He will deliver!

While being in a day treatment program of CMH I was offered to work at Goodwill. They had a program there for disabled individuals to make small parts. I remember putting o-rings in a tiny part. I put all my energy into making these parts. And making them good. I wanted to be better and I decided working with my hands as fast as I could would lead me in the right direction, of being in Christ's will. I believed it would set me free of the visions and voices I heard. And it was a good start in my healing.

It helped me to focus better and more often. Although I still had symptoms and plenty of fear I needed to overcome. I believe it was a big start in doing what was right for Christ. And I was better able to function.

Every little step helps in becoming functional and being able to manage the schizophrenia and not having it manage you.

"I cry"

As I write I cry I put my family through a lot. When someone would do something that hurt me, I'd call home and go on and on about it. I did not know how to temper my language and I'd be very vocal. "They did this", "they did that".

One day I was driving with my Mom and she said I'd go on and on about things and she didn't know what to do.

I was too vehement in my presentation of what had happened to me (the wrong I felt happened) and I came off looking irrational.

I thought about this conversation with my Mom for some time and I realized what I was looking for from her was to acknowledge what I was saying. Just to hear someone say "I'm sorry that happened to you", I think now would have stopped my ranting on and on about it. But knowing the height of fear schizophrenia has with it, they may have to say it a few times. But I see why she didn't know what to do because I was so vehement.

What I'm saying I guess is don't let your gander get up so high you scream everyone away! God isn't going to leave you with nothing. He takes care of His own. Remember that, confess that. Go straight to the throne room and tell Him He promised and you expect it. That is your right!

Of course if you are a friend of a person with schizophrenia, "I'm sorry that happened to you", might just do. And understand it is fear talking too.

"My Stories"

I read a book called "Some Kind of Miracle" by Iris Rainer Dart. It was a fiction story about a woman with schizophrenia. The author did such a good job of portraying this woman with the disorder. And while reading it I felt a sense of calm. Prior to reading it I had felt like going into the hospital again. And while reading it the desire left me. I don't know why but just hearing about someone going through some crazy situations like this woman did brought calm to me. Reading her story even though fictitious it calmed me!

I could see how crazy her life was and just seeing that calmed me and my fears. So I decided to write synopsis of my story in the next few pages for that reason. Plus there are helpful tips in them as well.

My Story

I got upset, fearful, my husband said he wanted to leave me two days ago. The words taunt me, he changed his mind. But I get confused. It is hard to breathe. I shouldn't be here in this house. This isn't the right place for me to be. I grab a coat and run out the door.

I'm walking, a fast gate, down the side of the street. I come to an area with sidewalks and I continue crying inside. He doesn't want me. I can't go home. I'm all alone. I run a ways. Where will I go. Who will help me.

No one, I know that. There is no where for me to go. I've turned my family and friends against me. There is no where to go. Crying inside, I walk. I'm tired, I slow down.

I see dog barf on the side walk. The voices tell me I need to eat it to be saved. I won't be saved if I don't. I bend down and take some . . .

I'm home, he is home; my husband that is. I tell him I ate dog barf today. Oh, and he walks away.

I will not do that again, he helped me in that way by his indifference to what I had said and because he let me alone with it. Others would have locked me away and I may have continued the behavior. I thank God for my husband of that day.

My Story Two

I believe sex was wrong. People shouldn't be doing that for fun. It is something you do to have babies. Why does he want sex, my husband that is. I don't get it. It is so hard for me. What is it all about. It isn't right.

Nude, I run out the door and down the street as if someone were chasing me. I weave back and forth, like a deer caught in a head light, yet there are no cars. He is in the front yard when I look back. Head hung he walks in circles. I'm still running wild like a deer. I turn a corner and see a family sitting on their porch. I turn back and run for the neighbors house.

I knock on their door and she comes to the door. Oh, did he put you out. Yes I say, after all what was this desire he has. She gets me a robe and says bring it back when your done with it. I go home, walk in and change and return the robe.

He is my husband and that is what marriage is all about. I made it through another crazy day with others constant love and care for me in a time of crisis. I learned through their caring that it is ok to be a wife and they didn't lock me up or put me away, so I no longer want to run wild in the street. I thank God for a precious neighbor and for my husband.

My Story Three

Every day I clean the house. I want to be a good housewife. I wash walls and change everything around. He, my husband comes home. And I tell him "I ate a fly today". He looks at me and says you know maggots come from flies.

Well, I guess I will not be doing that again! I thought Jesus wanted me to do it. In reality: his (Jesus') yoke is easy, and His Burden is light. Where was that verse when I needed it! It sure wasn't easy eating that fly or the barf earlier when I thought Jesus wanted me to. Since it was not easy I know now it was not Jesus that wanted me to do it! And by my husband letting it go and his one comment, I am free from that burden as well.

That is another commanding verse that came in handy with my schizophrenia. "His yoke is easy, and His burden light". So I would say not so, His yoke is easy and His burden light so leave me alone! It is not wrong to look to Christ to deliver us as schizophrenics. So many times the people helping us would tell us not to speak about Christ. Of all people in the world He is, the only one who can deliver us and when we look to His word, we find our deliverance.

My Story Four

My husband and I were up north, in Michigan, at a cabin owned by his Step Mom. We are vacationing, spending time together. I'm having trouble with my body aching all over and it makes it hard for me to walk. He takes my arm and helps me along. I don't know why I feel this way but I do.

We are walking to the lake and back and my voices interfered, you won't be saved unless you pee right now. I continue walking and I pee right then. My husband continues to hold my arm and help me along back to the cabin not saying a word. I get cleaned up and change my clothes. We continue with our vacation.

What was that verse again? His (Jesus') yoke is easy, and His burden is light. That sure was not an easy thing to do either and I'm thankful my husband turned the other way again as I've been delivered from this as well.

His yoke is easy and His burden is light. Don't forget that verse and use it when ever you hear a voice speaking to your something off the wall you don't want to do. It is the enemy of our souls not Our LORD and Savior, Jesus Christ.

My Story Five

Another day, I am angry about all the sex and violence on TV. My whole life I've been subjected to and put in fear by the shows on television. I think of Madonna and how she acts and dresses. So I get a brainy idea. I take off my clothes except for my underpants, pad and bra. I put on a hooded jacket and I head out the front door. I'll show them? I walk to the neighbor's house and knock on their door. The house is empty but the landlord and his wife are there along with their helper. The helper runs out the back door. I feel bad for what I've done but I continue on out the front door and down the street. Next I walk in the front door of the neighborhood restaurant. Then right back out. I know the police are coming now, and that is just punishment for upsetting my landlord's helper and my friend. I'm walking down the street bare footed and there are puddles I have to skip over. I'm surrounded by police cars. I stop and they talk with me. I tell them I like Madonna. Well I do. But I don't like the sex and violence on television or from her. I don't tell them that though. They tell me Madonna does that on stage and that it isn't appropriate to wear stuff like that on the street. And if I want to dress like that I need to stay in my house. I understand and they escort me home. I'm thankful to God for His great wisdom and love in showing me what is right and wrong in these situations, through family and Officials. Again, where was that verse when I needed it?

My Story Six

Oh my, I believed I was the worst sinner in the world! But really, all people are sinners! Everyone sins in one way or another every day. Not that they want to it just happens.

That is so good I need to say it again: Really, all people are sinners!

I was sexually immoral for most of the years of my growing up life. If you have schizophrenia, I bet you have too. And too, you probably believe your un-savable because of it. A lot of people sin, you can be forgiven. I quit being sexually immoral. Then I got married and being with my husband (where the bed is undefiled) I felt wrong and I also got back into sexual immorality. I didn't want to and every time I did I called out to Jesus: Deliver me!

He did. With my husband's constant care and unwavering strength to do right in the marriage, I was delivered. See, God does love me. He loves you too. Be diligent in asking Christ to deliver you. You know what is right and wrong even if those helping you tell you it is alright. Jesus wants us to come to him as children and he will and does deliver. Just be diligent to ask him and He will.

I know a lot of people smoke too and feel condemned because of that too. Jesus knows! He can deliver you, just continue to seek Him for your deliverance. He will change you. He did me.

My Story Seven

I was in the psychiatric ward in one of my bad spells and my parents came up to visit me as they always did. That support was immeasurable. I needed that even though they couldn't handle me at home and it was hard.

Well this particular visit we were talking and drinking water and I took the glass of drinking water and threw it in my Mom's face. I was fearful they were not saved and I was going to baptize them no matter what. Dad looked at me and firmly said "you better not!" He knew what I was about to do. Of course I was going to baptize him too.

I was so fearful for them, but by him directing me what to do I was able to forget about it and not do it again.

As a caregiver, you need to take care of yourself too. If the only thing you can do is visit that is very important to the patient getting to a place where they can manage their day by themselves. Visitations are important, just to talk all the support and care that a visit brings is so helpful.

Don't think it is your fault you are sick. And if you are a caregiver, don't think it is your fault either. God allows things to happen for a purpose. You are NOT at fault. And you will not catch it either.

"Beautiful Smile"

Did you know you are beautiful
Did you know your smile touches
Many a heart
Giving warmth to others
Others in need
Others not in need
Friends
Acquaintances
Those you pass on every street of your life!

Your smile is beautiful
Your touch is warm and uplifting
People need you
Yes they need you
Your touch
Your smile
Your hand
To lift up others along the way

To be there on a sunny day
To be there on a not so sunny day
You are so important
To others existence
To other peoples lives

If you were no more
How would that light shine for me.

"You Are Beautiful" comes from a moment in time I cherish. We were having our annual garage sale and as always a family friend from Church stopped in to see what all we had. He smiled at me and he took his hand and squeezed my shoulder.

It was a smile of "you have touched my life". I smiled back and in that moment realized wow I touch other people's lives with my smile too. Just as they touch mine. I did not feel or know that before and that instance it became very real to me. I thought back over the years and all the friendly faces that touched my heart and how good that made me feel. And realized hey I touch others lives just the same. God's light shines through me too.

This young man from Church was rather popular and I was amazed that I could touch his life too, with just a smile. A beautiful smile.

Today I was transported back in time to another conversation with my friend a year ago. She was talking about suicide. Her own. Today she announced next year at this time she wouldn't be here any more. Everyone told her don't talk like that. But I sat and remembered our conversation. See I was suicidal before and I knew a trick that could help her and I told it to her. I was saddened by my misgiving of information after the fact and then this year at Christmas time again, I fear for her safety.

Katie Hartwig

What we all need to know is we touch other peoples lives. For good. In this dark world where the deceiver lives we are the light of Christ that keeps other people going. We are needed and most times in just that small way.

I learned if someone commits suicide in a family, it is more likely that others will as well. How sad is that. How many tears can we cry for them. How can we make life better, with a smile. One smile is contagious. Sadly one suicide is too.

How would you feel if someone you loved killed themselves. Yes it would hurt. I know one of my buddies did exactly that just a few years out of school. He was one of those important smiles to me. He touched my life and then he was gone.

Don't you see we all need to go on. To be there for others to be that smile and to share that light in this crazy world. One smile by one smile the world becomes a better place. And when Christ shines through you like that, it will be a better place.

Don't give up, don't give in, you have much more to give. You are needed. Think about what I have said, so many people would hurt if you were to commit suicide. And others might follow you.

Be a light, be a Beautiful smile.

"Suicide"

Suicide is against the law.
Did you know that?
I didn't know it.
Police come and write
A report up on you when
You try to do that.

It is really against the law!

You can not ask yourself too much:

How did you feel so bad?
How did you get so empty?
What did you do that for?

In so doing, you may just be delivered from the urge
to commit suicide as well.

In thinking about suicide, I thought I was making life
easier for family and friends. That is not so. I found
over the years it is an angry act against the very
people you think you are protecting.

So my friend, why suicide?

"Suicide" is a sad side affect of a person who has schizophrenia. They can become despondent and it leads to suicide. I was suicidal for many years. It is something people don't like to talk about but here I am.

I did not know it was illegal. Just that realization helped me to know it was the wrong thing to do. After three serious attempts I found this out.

I felt I was the worst sinner in the world. I felt like I did no right. That I hurt people. That my sins were taking me to hell and that if I committed suicide I would stop the sinning. I would stop it and the world would be a better place without me.

This was all wrong. Jesus Christ died for the sinner. He was perfect and when we ask Him into our lives, His righteousness becomes our righteousness. I went to a counselor who was part of "The Exchange Life". That is what it is all about: we exchange our sin for Christ's righteousness. I did not know that. And I also thought if I keep sinning after I've accepted Christ I was horrible. That is wrong! Christ knows we are sinners and all we need to do is stop and say sorry for it and it is no longer our sin. Every day is a new day in Christ. A new day for you! Yes you, and for myself as well. Christ teaches us how to do right. He gives us the tools to move forward to change.

Most people involved with schizophrenic people tell them they can not talk about God. We need Him, and His laws, they help us become a person who can stand on our own.

"Pep Talk"

Hello dear friend,

You see things, you think are wrong and you don't understand. You feel you keep doing wrong and no one else does. You blame yourself, hold yourself to what you've done wrong. Stop, everyone does wrong. That is why Jesus died. He doesn't remember your sins; really they are forgiven!

You know them, every one of them. But you don't have to. It is alright, Jesus died for your sins, for all your sins. And if you haven't ask yet ask Him: "Jesus forgive me, come into my heart and change me, I love you and thank You, Amen". Now, He died for your sins. You are perfect in Him. He was righteous and in Him you are too. You don't have to keep the wrongs they are gone—AS FAR AS THE EAST IS FROM THE WEST: Gone! That is another promise in the bible. Say sin you are gone as far as the east is from the west, gone. Leave me alone!

So don't think on your sin or remember them any more. IF they come back to you say: so what, I did that before, but I'm not any more., so leave me alone you deceiver: I am white as snow because of Jesus, God's loving grace! Maybe you smoke or have sexual sin and you want to stop because you are in bondage, again he will deliver you just be diligent to seek Him and ask Him for deliverance. He will.

"Pep Talk Two"

I had trouble feeling condemned all the time. Oh my every sin I ever did would bombard me. Thoughts would come to me that I wasn't saved because I did this or that and that I was not savable.

1. THE DECEIVER IS THE ACCUSER OF (THE BRETHERN)

   Think of that "the deceiver"—Not GOD!

2. GOD came to save us!

Satan is the accuser of "the Brethren""
   If he is accusing you,
      YOU must be part of the brethren.

And a very special part, I might add, if he is trying to condemn you so badly.

God forgives your sins. Now just tell the deceiver to back off. Yeah sure you did that before, but your not going to do it again. Tell him you are forgiven and in Jesus you are clean!

White as the driven snow, that is how clean. White as snow.

"Pep Talk Three"

I believe all schizophrenic people feel responsible for other people around them. They feel they need to take care of them. But they don't know how. They see things that other people do wrong and they are fearful for the other person. Most times being overwhelmed by taking on others problems and their own. They see things they have done and want to condemn themselves. But oddly they want to fix it for others. It is not our place to take care of other people—STOP.

If you see other people's sins you're accountable for them. DON'T BE DISMAYED: Ask Jesus to help you so you don't. He will forgive even that. And if I see someone sin I say "that is none of my business" and "it may not be a sin for them". It might just be my interpretation. We don't have to take care of other people. It is not our place. Our job is to take care of ourselves first with God's help and others around us. And it is our job to forgive ourselves as God has already!
Be nice to yourself.
Be nice to those around you.
WE ALL deserve it.
Continue to ask our Great God for deliverance of things you feel are Wrong.
It does say in the bible to be a little righteous and a little wicked.
So as Auntie says "Whatever floats your boat!".

"Pep Talk for smokers"

Well this may be just a bit radical, but I'll say it anyway. Why do you condemn yourself for smoking. I haven't read anywhere in the bible where it says you smoke your going to hell.

It just isn't there.

True it says if you eat something that is not good for you it is wrong. But smoking is not eating.

Smoking is not against the law, it is legal in the United States of America and probably in most Countries.

I know there are many people in Churches who smoke. Sure they may wonder, is God going to forgive me for that. But too all people should wonder and hope as well to be saved. I don't believe it is a given for any one person. We are all hoping on THE LORD and you should too. If you feel smoking is wrong, ask Jesus to deliver you. He will, He is good that way.

So yes, you too can be saved. If you're feeling condemned, you must be very special to Jesus for the deceiver to want to condemn you so much. So think on that!

"Pep talk for those who are suicidal"

Right now you probably feel like life is so hard, and no one cares about you and that you have committed the unpardonable sin, and that you might as well just do it. You think that you are saving the world from you hurting it or other people more. That is how I felt. I knew I had sinned and I let "The deceiver" talk me into believing I was not savable and just do it. It didn't work. Why? I think Jesus wanted me and so I'm here today! Maybe just to write this book to help one more person?

I still had feelings of suicide for quite come times after I tried, I can not lie. How I turned those feelings around was some what easy after I did it and I hope what I did might help you as well.

I began singing a song over and over that had some questions about suicide. The song is by Blaine Larson, a Country singer: "How do you feel so empty."

What good questions. And as I sang the songs over and over again, I would think about a friend of mine who was suicidal too. And in so doing God delivered me from the desire. He sure is good.

By the cd and add "How do you feel so empty" to your box of music!

When I sang it no one knew what I was thinking. I was thinking of a friend I knew who was suicidal asking these questions as I sang. At the time it was a very popular song and on the radio three to four times a day. So it was easy to sing along to. And I had a working buddy who loved the song too and we'd sing it together, every time it was on. I did it more then once and continued to do it. Then I began to feel free from the nagging thoughts that had tormented me since I was eleven.
I had done something wrong at that age.

It caused me pain for years. But Jesus set me free. By me simply asking these questions in song. I believe He will set you free as well. His mercies are new every day. We as schizophrenic people don't seem to realize those mercies. We are too busy beating ourselves up over things we did in the past. It is time to forget. Jesus has, and we can too. HIS MERCIES ARE NEW EVERY DAY.

That means YOU can be forgiven no matter how bad you feel you have sinned. Remember everyone sins and most probably every day. You just need to ask for forgiveness and try not to do it again. And those sins where you feel bound, seek deliverance from Christ over and over if you need to. He is faithful to deliver.

"Critical"

I have found that I am too critical. Well I guess that has already been put across but it is good to know. If you are schizophrenic as I've said you probably are too. We tend to see things that other people do that is wrong. And coupled with being critical we want to fix it. We get dismayed by this great need to want to be perfect; or having things perfect around us. News flash, nothing will be perfect until Christ returns and makes it that way.

1. Things will not be perfect until Christ returns
2. That is biblical, don't try to fix it.

Once you realize "yeah, we are all sinners", then you will feel better. Of course we don't try to sin, most people want to do right and for the most part they do.

If sin creeps in and we catch it, we stop it. We ask Jesus to forgive us and we go on. We don't have to pay for every little sin we have committed. And neither does anyone else.

I'll say that again: You don't have to pay for every little sin you have committed. Jesus already paid the price for our sins. And the sins of others as well.

1. Things will not be perfect until Jesus return
2. That is biblical, don't try to fix it.
3. And what a great day that will be.

"Another Kind of Serenity Prayer"— "The Courage Prayer"

I had been to many different support groups in my life and had heard the Serenity Prayer but it never gave me comfort. I didn't understand it and could not feel its power. Until one day a co-worker gave me the prayer to give to another friend of mine. I knew the prayer, But, I asked her to tell it to me again and I wrote it out as she repeated it to me so I could give it to my friend.

As I walked away from this friend I looked at the prayer myself and I thought: "God grant me the "Courage" to accept the things I can not change. The serenity to change the things I can and the wisdom to know the difference".

All these years the prayer made no sense to me and in this moment it transformed me. And I felt a peace I had not felt before. All I needed was the courage to accept I couldn't change the situation. It was as thought Jesus stepped down and put his hand upon my shoulder and calmed my fears.

My fears for one thing at the time was my other friend. I feared for her life and for her job she had just lost and I wanted to fix it and in my mind I was trying to fix it. And in that moment when I said the prayer,

The Courage Prayer; my heart became content and I knew I couldn't fix the situation for this friend I cared so much about and I had the courage to accept that. I believe many people with schizophrenia have this problem. They want so much to make it right for people they know that they over load themselves and can not function in return. And in reality they become the one in need and they look to be selfish and self centered. When all it is, is that they need "the courage prayer"!

"Schizophrenia The Other Side"

Schizophrenia,
Looking in you see a person
Who is self centered and selfish.

Looking out we see a need and we
Don't know how to fix it.

We want SO much to fix it
For ourselves and for others
That we get lost in it

Schizophrenia,
Hearing things
Seeing things

All because
We became distraught
Over wanting to fix it
And in turn we become
So confused
We breakdown
And we become lazy
Looking in the wrong direction.

"Encouragement"

Give heart dear friend
Jesus loves you
And can save you and
If you have already asked, he has.
You can be delivered
From voices and seeing things.

Use the helpful tips
In this book
Work as hard as you can
With your hands
Focus on what you are doing.
Ask Jesus, to forgive you
And come into your life.
Know that doesn't make you
Perfect all at once or stop you
From sinning.
Everyone sins every day
Just ask for forgiveness and go on
Direct the deceiver to get off
Not so!
No I don't care to hear that!
Not so I don't care to see that!
You ARE a precious child of God
We all are
Thank God.

"My Voices"

My voice's
They won't leave

I hear thing taunting me
Condemning me
Threatening me
Where did they come from
I may never know

But they are there
In the black of the night
In day light too

I hear them taunting me

Go away, I say, GO AWAY
I don't want to hear leave me alone
I don't want to hear STOP

That is all I have to say
And it works
More and more each day
Along with my right meds of course!

"KEEP SEEKING A DOCTOR"

Keep seeking a doctor who will listen to you. I was told many times I just did not want to take my meds. Yeah, that was partly true: I wanted to take meds but the side affects were worse then the schizophrenia. After many years and many hospitalizations I finally found a med that worked and didn't cause me terrible side affects. And I am so grateful to God for that. He really is a good God. Funny thing is, it was the same medication I had such terrible pain from in earlier years. So keep trying, keep trying.

I also found out that sublingual B helped me. I buy it at the local Meijer's it is a liquid and I put it under my tongue for 30 seconds then swallow. That took away the visions I would see even on a medication.

I heard about sublingual B on a TV Paid program ad. The doctor was talking about when he was an intern and the doctor who was teaching him taught him this trick. There was an elderly gentleman admitted to the hospital. He was yelling and being very disoriented. The doctor said I'll have him all fixed up in a couple of days, "watch this." He gave him Vitamin B shots and within a week he was back to normal and walking out of the hospital with his family.

When I saw the ad I thought, maybe that is my problem. Maybe I need B. I found it at Meijers in the vitamin section in a liquid form. I was ever so happy when it worked and that it only costed around six dollars.

"Instruction"

When your friend or acquaintance
Is going through something difficult
Don't be distraught

When your friend is having a hard day
And can not cope
Don't be distraught

Sometimes people go through though times with
God so HE can change them and bless them and
help them to be stronger in HIM, so they will know
HIS will. So He can perform a good work for them.
Maybe not right away but He will. He said He will.

Take heart dear friend
Don't be distraught
Don't think you have to fix it
God really does have your friend in His hand
And He will take care of them
He said He would and He will

So often we think we need to fix it for someone
That is NOT our job
Take heart my friend, He said He will.

And being so upset over it all, never works out now
does it!

"Dear Friend why suicide"

Why suicide dear friend

God's mercies are new each morning
He forgives us our sins,
If we forgive others their sins.

His mercies are new each morning
Things will be different tomorrow.
Take heart dear friend.
Maybe someone did not call
They might tomorrow?
And just maybe you will find
Hey I don't want to talk
To that person anyway

Seriously, new people come
Into our lives
Every day and it is ok.

Why suicide dear one
It is against the law
And you can be forgiven
This lonely time
This lonely hour will pass

God's mercies are new each morning

"Buck naked"

Did you know running buck naked in the street is illegal.
WELL IT IS.
Did you now even in the bible it was considered evil
Adam and Eve knew that they were naked after they ate
Noah's son Ham saw him naked and told his brothers
And that son was cursed because of it

I thought God made us that way and that is what
I should do I couldn't figure out why other people
didn't do it too.

I ran down the street a couple times as I said. And
when I met up with the police they told me it is illegal.

It really is illegal!

And God didn't make us this way to walk around this
way. As a matter of fact God made Adam and Eve
clothes of skin to cover them, He doesn't want us
walking around naked.

It truly is illegal and evil.

God even banished us from the Garden of Eden
because we knew it was evil. Once again: His yoke
is easy, and His burden light. And that sure is not
easy to do, now is it. It really was hard for me to

do. If you find you are addicted to this habit, once again seek Christ for deliverance. He will deliver you. Remember again everyone sins and you can and are forgiven.

"Yeah I sinned"

Yeah, I sinned
But it isn't hopeless

Everyone sins
Did you know that?

And it isn't hopeless
Jesus died for our sins

We can be forgiven
If we ask for it
Forgive us LORD for our sins

It is not hopeless!
You are forgiven

Seeking Jesus is alright
He will bring you through
He will deliver you too
Jesus come into my life
And deliver me
And he will
It is not hopeless

Take heart dear friend
It is not hopeless.

"Accuser of the brethren"

Jesus is not "the accuser of the brethren". If you are feeling accused it is not God; I always thought it was, but it isn't. If your feeling accused it is "the deceiver" he wants to accuse you to make you do wrong (even make your commit suicide).

Jesus is not "the accuser" so don't be fooled.

I don't want to be fooled any more. Some days are harder then others to remember this because the deceiver keeps knocking at my door telling me I did wrong, telling me I'm going to hell anyway, nagging, nagging, nagging me. That is not God!

We all just need to remember Jesus is not "the accuser". Jesus doesn't come to accuse us, He came to save us! In Jesus we are saved.

So don't be fooled any more. Everybody sins. That is why it is called grace. He laid down His life to cover your sins. Not to accuse you.

When you feel accused tell the old deceiver to "Buzz off"! Yeah maybe I did that in the past but no more. I am free by the grace of God. Jesus covers my sins. I won't do that any more. If you feel your still sinning, proclaim Jesus will deliver me. Then tell that old deceiver: I don't want to hear that leave me alone! I don't want to see that leave me alone. Take a stand! Continue to ask our Loving Father to deliver you, HE will.

"Let Me Be"

Why don't you let me be
So I'm different
So I say and think differently
That doesn't' mean I'm wrong
At least not to me
My reality is different
I'm me, you are you
So I say things you don't like
Just listen
That is all
Don't judge me
Tie me up
Lock me up
Medicate me
I don't mind medication if it works
But most don't
Can't you see
I just need to be me
Even if you don't understand
Let me be
So I am free to grow
To know the truth in time
Help me find the right medication
Help me be me

This poem comes from my heart. I learned to be more like you by being me for a time. My husband just listened to me. He didn't put me away. He just sat quietly. He just listened to me and in so doing I grew and now I know most of what I said when I was distraught was crazy sounding. I just needed to be me as I was at the time. And now I am free from those crazy thoughts and ideas.

Well, mostly free. Some thoughts I still have as beliefs of mine and I have decided, they are my thoughts and I don't share them with others. I realize people don't always want to hear my thoughts. And what does it hurt to have different beliefs; I just don't expect others to understand, like I use to.

"Making my delusions work for me at my job"

Being schizophrenic and working can have its advantages. I work in a factory and most times it can be boring to those who work. But I've found in my mind I can make things livelier then most.

For instance when I'm loading the parts in the box to ship to plating, I put them in 6 at a time and 3 sets. As I'm loading them, I'm thinking in my schizophrenic mind that the parts can hear my thoughts and can respond to me. It makes my time go by faster at work and I chuckle inside about it. They sometimes have races and certain parts want to be first in the box. Some like to be in the middle. Some fight over the first spot and some trick other parts to get the first spot. I pretend they are talking to me and I to them. And I chuckle with those who win the race! Well it can be entertaining. I take it back to the scripture I read, that in the latter days if no one praises God the rocks will cry out in praise and so I take it a few steps farther and I have my entertainment for the day.

There was a time when I didn't know this was just a game. A time when I was so involved with "the rocks crying out"! But since I've been on the right meds and have been through a lot of counsel and understanding; I know I am just playing a game to entertain me in a boring day. You got to admit it is pretty funny! Sometimes too create faces in the cement floor for a smile too can be fun, I just don't dwell on it.

I don't have to do this any more as I've grown in Christ. And I am thankful to God for delivering me from this as well. Then I read and found out this was wrong to do as well. It was great He delivered me from this before I read about it. :O)

"Working with My Dad"

My Dad passed away 13 years ago and he use to weld when he was alive. I would go with him to work and He would always say, "Don't look at the flame it will ruin your eyes." Now, I'm the one brazing and it makes me feel closer to him. I like to think of him as my angel, as I work. And I like to think of it as Him and I working together. That God's purpose in taking my Dad and my brother was to have them working in heaven preparing a place for you and me. They were so talented. I like to dream it helps me through the day. This way I make a mundane day into one that is kind of exciting and joyful to do. I can praise God for all His blessings to me, especially my job.

Letter to a friend or relative

Yes, I may need meds to get me through.
But no they all don't work for me.
Yes, the right med is hard to find, be patient.

Sublingual B took away all the floating images for me.
You can buy it in liquid form at Meijer's for $6.

Yes, I can talk about God. And I know I sin BUT He forgives me, even daily sometimes. All I need to do is tell him I'm sorry and my mistake is erased. Yours are too!

Yes, I know I sin. But now I know how to be delivered, ask Jesus for forgiveness and try to be the best I can for HIM.

Don't freak out over something crazy I might say, just listen.
Don't comment, just be there. Or be indifferent if you do speak. Like a child, I feel accepted that way. And I will learn in time hey that was crazy too.

If you have to put me in the hospital, visit as often as you can. And give me change so I can call you too.

A Song

Save me Oh LORD with your righteous right hand change
my heart, change me Oh LORD, to glorify Thee.
Change me Oh LORD to glorify Thee.

I can not do this alone
I can not change on my own
Save me Oh LORD heal my heart
My mind, my soul
Direct my eyes to see what is pure, lovely, right and true

Change me Oh LORD to glorify Thee
Only in Your presence will I totally be free

I need You, I live You, and I want to be free

Save me Oh LORD and teach me.

To seek to be like You
Meek and lowly in heart
Not judging others
Being meek and lowly in heart

Guard my eyes Jesus, that I may not see bad.
Guard my heart LORD Jesus, that I may worship Thee.
Make me pure Oh LORD as You are pure.
Save me Oh LORD and teach me too.

"A Prayer"

Father in Heaven we adore you
For you alone are worthy of our adoration and praise
We come before you Jesus
Asking that you tend to all people everywhere
We all need you
Let your perfect will be done in each and every life
We pray for our leaders Oh LORD,
That they would rule with love and with peace
As only you can cause this to be
We pray oh LORD that you would forgive us our sins
And teach us to love others as you would want us too
Not in our way but only in Yours
We thank you LORD that you have given us a new day
That your mercies are new each day and that our sins are
Forgiven each day through You
We thank you LORD for those reading this book and the
Tender care it may generate for those truly in need of Your
Constant love and Your touch.
We Pray all this in the name of Jesus.
Amen.

"It is great to have someone who experiences this illness to express how people can help themselves or a loved one."

I have read Katie Hartwig's book "Schizophrenia The Voices, they won't let me go . . . or will they". I feel it is a very good book and would recommend it to anyone who has schizophrenia, and also for their families so they might better understand how to help their loved one. It has a lot of good ideas. It is great to have someone who experiences this illness to express how people can help themselves or a loved one. I love you and am proud of your accomplishments. Mom

"The word schizophrenia is more than most of us can visualize or comprehend and this book opens that world for all to see and feel."

Anyone who has plans to read "Schizophrenia" The Voices, They Won't Let Go . . . or will they? by Katie Hartwig will realize the terror, frustration and since of being lost that the writer experienced. The word schizophrenia is more than most of us can visualize or comprehend and this book opens that world for all to see and feel. I recommend this book to anyone that questions nature as to why some of us are challenged much more than others.